12|15

COGGESHALL
TO RENEW

D0835795

Please return this book on or before the date shown above. To renew go to www.essex.gov.uk/libraries, ring 0345 603 7628 or go to any Essex library.

Essex County Council

THE MAYA AND OTHER AMERICAN CIVILISATIONS

BY CHARLIE SAMUELS

W

FRANKLIN WATTS
LONDON•SYDNEY

First published in Great Britain in 2015 by
The Watts Publishing Group

Copyright © 2015 Brown Bear Books Ltd

For Brown Bear Books Ltd:
Editorial Director: Lindsey Lowe
Managing Editor: Tim Cooke
Children's Publisher: Anne O'Daly
Art Director: Jeni Child
Designer: Lynne Lennon
Picture Manager: Sophie Mortimer

Dewey no. 972

ISBN: 978 1 4451 4259 3

Printed in China

Franklin Watts
An imprint of
Hachette Children's Group
Part of the Watts Publishing Group
Carmelite House
50 Victoria Embankment
London EC4Y 0DZ

An Hachette UK company
www.hachette.co.uk

www.franklinwatts.co.uk

CONTENTS

INTRODUCTION

Centuries before Europeans arrived in the Americas, peoples such as the Aztecs, Inca and Maya were outstanding builders. When the first Spaniards arrived early in the 16th century, they were astonished at the cities of the Aztecs and Inca. Many early American cultures did not build in stone. They left few records. But in the deserts of what is now the Southwestern United States, in the jungles of Mesoamerica (southern Mexico and Central America)

The Maya built this tomb for King Pakal in the city of Palenque in southern Mexico during the seventh century CE.

and in the Andes Mountains, people achieved high levels of craftsmanship. Innovation helped them adapt to what were often hostile environments. Technology gradually changed in a series of tiny improvements, rather than in great steps.

THREE MIGHTY EMPIRES

This book covers a period from about 1000 BCE to about 1550 CE. It concentrates on the empires of the Maya and Aztecs of Mexico, and the Inca of Peru. The Maya Empire declined by the ninth century CE. The later empires of the Aztecs and Inca lasted until the Spaniards arrived in Mexico in 1519 and in Peru in 1532. Weakened by political division and facing gunpowder weapons, the empires fell. This book will introduce you to examples of the remarkable technology used in the Americas before the Europeans arrived.

TECHNOLOGICAL BACKGROUND

Compared with other ancient civilisations, those of the Americas began relatively late. But before the great Aztec and Inca empires arose in the 15th and 16th centuries, other civilisations had achieved high levels of technological accomplishment. They included the Maya, whose culture began as early as 1500 BCE. It had largely vanished by the middle of the ninth century CE. The Aztecs and Inca drew on the technology of earlier peoples. The Aztecs, for example, adapted the Mayan calendar and forms of Mayan writing.

The Olmec carved huge heads in rock. The heads may represent people who played a sacred ball game.

The pyramids of Teotihuacán in Mexico date from the first century CE. Over 1,400 years later, the Aztecs believed they had been built by the gods.

OLMEC, TOLTEC AND MOCHE

The Olmec of Mexico (1200 BCE–400 CE) built large earth mounds to serve as ceremonial centres. They transported huge boulders without any wheeled transport, probably by using rafts on lakes and rivers. Later peoples built stone pyramids instead of mounds. The Toltec (c.900–1200 CE) built their capital city of Tula in central Mexico around a stepped temple pyramid. They also built huge basalt statues, known as *chacmools*. The Moche of Peru flourished between the second and eighth centuries. They grew crops and built canals to irrigate them. They travelled in reed boats. Such technology was also used by the Aztecs and Inca.

FARMING

Life in Mesoamerica was based on farming. When the Spaniards arrived, the Mesoamericans were some of the world's most advanced farmers. They grew food plants that were later introduced to the rest of the world, such as the potato. Corn (maize) was the most important crop. It was used as food and to make beer.

Harvesting corn

Woollen papoose to carry baby

Early corn cobs were only 2.5 cm (1 inch) long (left). It took 5,000 years of farming for the modern cob to appear (right).

Stone-bladed axe to harvest crops

> The American peoples bred many different varieties of corn, which grew even at high altitudes in the Andes.

How people farmed depended on where they lived. In the highlands, the Inca used terracing to farm on the steep mountainsides. In the Mexican lowlands, the Aztecs reclaimed land from swamps and lakes by making *chinampas*. These were built-up beds of fertile earth on top of a base of reeds. The Aztec planted seeds using a *uictli* (digging stick).

MAYA FARMING

The Maya built drainage canals in the Yucatán and made raised beds like the Aztec *chinampas*. They turned the soil with digging sticks and stone-bladed hoes. They planted corn (maize) on the ridges in the soil, with beans and squash in the furrows in between.

TECHNICAL SPECS

- None of the Mesoamerican cultures used ploughs. Farmers turned the soil with digging sticks made from strong wood.
- The Aztecs had no draught animals to carry loads. They relied on human labour.
- The Maya boiled corn with lime or ground-up snail shells to increase the amount of niacin in the corn. A lack of niacin can cause a vitamin deficiency called pellagra.
- The Inca preserved potatoes by freezing them. They left the potatoes out overnight to freeze. During the day, when the potatoes thawed, people walked on them to squeeze out moisture. After a few days, the potatoes (or *chuño*) were ready to be stored for up to a year.

TERRACES AND IRRIGATION

These narrow terraces were built by the Inca at the city of Machu Picchu, high in the Andes Mountains.

For the Inca who lived high up in the Andes, the soil was poor and the ground was too steep to grow crops. To solve the problem, the Inca built flat terraces on the steep mountainsides. The Inca and other American peoples also built canals for irrigation.

As well as creating more land for crops, the terraces helped prevent erosion of the soil by wind or rain. The Inca dug narrow steps into the mountainside. The steps were supported by stone walls.

CANAL BUILDING

To irrigate the terraces, the Inca built canals along the contours of the slopes. In North America, the Hohokam of the Sonoran Desert (c.200–1400 CE) built canals to irrigate their fields. They used weirs to control the flow of the water from the Gila River.

TECHNICAL SPECS

- At the peak of the Inca Empire in the 16th century CE, terraces covered 10,000 square kilometres (3,860 square miles).
- The stone retaining walls helped to keep the soil warm during cold nights. This helped to extend the growing season.
- Inca terraces conserved water well. The soil stayed damp for six months after rain.
- The Inca mixed the soil with small stones to prevent the soil expanding after rain and pushing out the retaining walls.
- The Inca made mortar from a mixture of cement, lime, sand and water to build canals.

The Inca diverted rivers such as the Urubamba to water fields in the few flat-floored valleys.

MOUND BUILDING

By 1000 BCE, farming peoples had settled parts of North America. They still gathered wild plants, but they also grew crops. Some built huge earthworks, probably as tombs or for ceremonial purposes. Mound building continued for about 2,000 years. As many as 10,000 people lived in Cahokia, in present-day Illinois in the United States.

Serpent Mound may have had an astrological purpose. It seems to be aligned with the position of the Sun on certain days of the year.

At its peak in around 1100 CE, Cahokia had more than 100 mounds. The largest is Monk's Mound, a flat-topped structure with four terraces.

SERPENT MOUND

In what is now Ohio as long ago as 321 BCE, people built a mound shaped as a serpent following the curves of the land. The alignment of the snake's coils may have an astronomical meaning. At Emerald Mound in Mississippi, the Natchez people flattened a hill to make a large platform.

TECHNICAL SPECS

- The mound builders had no carts or pack animals. They had to carry the earth in baskets.
- Monk's Mound at Cahokia contains about 600,000 cubic metres (780,000 cubic yards) of earth.
- The flat platform on top of Emerald Mound held two flat-topped earth pyramids.
- The coils of Serpent Mound align with the position of the Sun during the equinoxes (when day and night are of equal length) and the solstices (the longest and shortest days of the year).

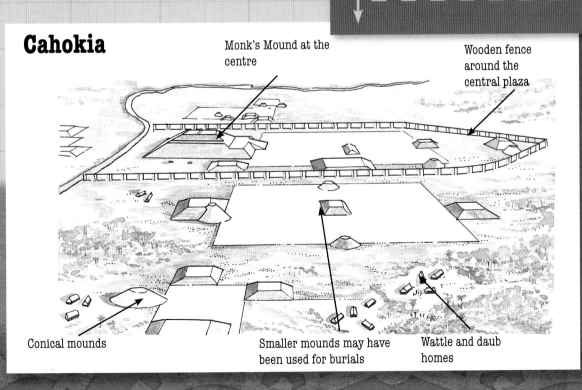

Cahokia

Monk's Mound at the centre

Wooden fence around the central plaza

Conical mounds

Smaller mounds may have been used for burials

Wattle and daub homes

PYRAMIDS AND ZIGGURATS

Thousands of years after the Egyptians built their pyramids, Mesoamerican peoples built ziggurats (stepped pyramids). The pyramids all had a religious purpose, but they are not related. The two cultures came up with the same solution to the problem of building tall structures.

The Maya built this pyramid at Chichén Itzá between the 9th and 12th centuries CE in honour of the god Kukulkán.

Teotihuacán

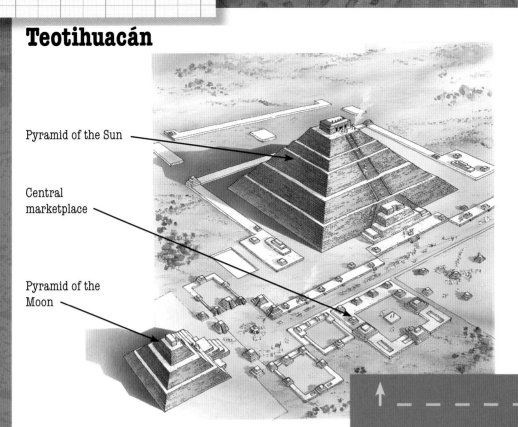

Pyramid of the Sun

Central marketplace

Pyramid of the Moon

SERIES OF PYRAMIDS

The Olmec built the earliest pyramid in the Americas in about 900 BCE at La Venta. Later, the Maya built pyramids from stone blocks with steep steps. The pyramids had temples at the top. In Teotihuacán, in Mexico, the Pyramid of the Sun and the Pyramid of the Moon were built in the first century CE. They stood on an avenue lined by smaller pyramids. The Aztecs built pyramids in the heart of their capital, Tenochtitlán. Priests used altars on top of the pyramids to sacrifice prisoners to the gods.

TECHNICAL SPECS

- Olmec pyramids represented the sacred mountain the Olmecs believed reached up to heaven.
- The Mayan city of Tikal had six tall pyramids, each with a temple on top.
- Mayan pyramids represented the three levels of the Maya universe: the underworld, the earthly world and the heavenly world.
- At Teotihuacán, human sacrifices were buried in the foundations of the Pyramid of the Moon.
- The Pyramid of the Sun at Teotihuacán is 64 metres (210 feet) tall; its base measures 220 by 232 metres (720 by 760 feet).

CLIFF HOUSES

Beneath a cliff in Canyon de Chelly, Arizona, the White House was home to a whole Anasazi community.

In the southwest of North America, the nomadic Anasazi learned to grow corn around the sixth century CE. That allowed them to form communities. The Anasazi settled in the region now known as the Four Corners, where the American states of Colorado, Arizona, New Mexico and Utah meet. They built their homes on cliffs for protection.

The early Anasazi lived in homes made from adobe (mud brick). Some were partly dug into the ground. By the 13th century CE, they lived in stone houses up to four storeys high. The houses had no windows or doors on the ground floor. Ladders led to entrances in the roof.

HOMES ON CLIFFS

At Mesa Verde, in Colorado, the Anasazi built homes in caves and overhangs in cliff faces. They accessed the houses by ladders. The builders had no metal tools. They shaped sandstone blocks for building by chipping them with harder stones from nearby riverbeds.

TECHNICAL SPECS

- Adobe bricks were made of sand, clay and water mixed with straw. The mixture was shaped using frames and dried in the sun.
- The Anasazi are known as the 'basketmakers' because they used baskets to cook in instead of clay or metal cooking pots.
- In Chaco Canyon, New Mexico, the 'great house' at Pueblo Bonito had as many as 800 rooms.
- At Mesa Verde, some ancient sites are high on cliffs. The Anasazi probably climbed to them using rope ladders or footholds carved into the rock.

The Cliff Palace at Mesa Verde is sheltered beneath an overhang. The round structures are ceremonial rooms named *kivas*.

PUEBLO BUILDING

Peoples in the Americas built their homes with materials that were easily available. In the lowlands of Mesoamerica and the deserts of the southwest, it rarely rains. Adobe (mud brick) was the main building material. The Aztec and Maya used stone for public buildings such as temples and palaces.

Taos Pueblo in New Mexico was built by the Taos people over 1,000 years ago. People have lived there ever since.

HOW TO...

Pueblo Bonito was the largest settlement in Chaco Canyon, New Mexico. It was built in a large D-shape, with its curved back facing the canyon wall, and could only be entered by ladder. It contained at least 800 joined rooms, built on several levels. It probably housed as many as 1,200 people at its height in the 12th century CE.

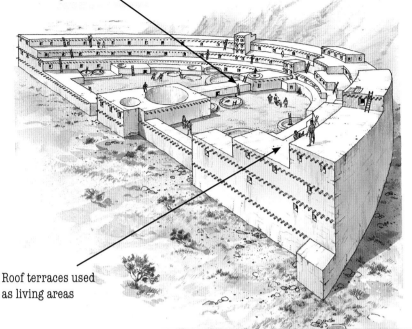

Central plaza with large *kivas*

Roof terraces used as living areas

The Aztecs built single-storey homes using adobe bricks made from sun-dried mud and straw. The houses had one big room with a roof of thatched straw.

PUEBLO PEOPLES

To the north, the Pueblo peoples were influenced by techniques from Mexico. The Anasazi built 'great houses', or large communal structures that each held many dwellings. The largest housed thousands of people. Access was by a system of ladders that led to doorways on the flat roofs. Circular pits named kivas, which were dug into the ground, were used for religious ceremonies.

TECHNICAL SPECS

- The Aztecs wove reed mats to sleep on the floor and built reed chests to store clothes. The Inca had no furniture.
- The Maya made plaster to line their pueblo homes by burning limestone for 36 hours to make a powder. They mixed the powder with water to make plaster.
- Pueblo Bonito's original gateway was narrowed and then blocked completely.
- The lower rooms in the pueblo had no windows. They were probably used for storage.

TENOCHTITLÁN

When the Spanish conquerors first saw the Aztec capital of Tenochtitlán, in 1519 CE, they could not believe their eyes. The city was far more sophisticated and larger than any European city. The city was laid out in a grid pattern. It had been built on swampy islands on Lake Texcoco in the Valley of Mexico.

This painting shows the ceremonial centre of Tenochtitlán and the causeways linking it to the shores of Lake Texcoco.

Double temple pyramid

Rack to display heads of human sacrifices

A View of Tenochtitlán

To build on the swampy land, the Aztecs created *chinampas* (mounds). They built them on reeds and mats weighted with stones and sunk between poles. On this base, the Aztecs piled mud from the lake to form a chinampa.

BUILDING ON AN ISLAND

The Aztecs built terracotta aqueducts to carry fresh water to the island. The island was accessed by three causeways. Only the centre of the island was strong enough to support stone structures. This was where the main temples and palaces were located. Ordinary people lived in one-roomed, one-storey adobe houses.

TECHNICAL SPECS

- The causeways had bridges in the middle that could be pulled up to defend the city.
- People used flat-bottomed canoes to travel around the city's canals.
- The Spaniards claimed that the causeways were wide enough for ten horses to walk abreast.
- The Templo Mayor in the heart of the city was rebuilt seven times. Each temple was built on top of the last. Its weight made it sink into the mud of Lake Texcoco.
- Modern-day Mexico City is built on the foundations of Tenochtitlán.
- The Aztec used human waste from public toilets to fertilise crops.

NAZCA LINES

The Nazca culture flourished in southern Peru between 100 BCE and 800 CE. The Nazca are best known for the massive drawings they made on the stony surface of the Nazca Desert. The purpose of these drawings remains a mystery. The Nazca were also skilled potters and textile makers.

This design is known as the hummingbird. Other images show familiar animals such as a whale and a monkey.

HOW TO...

The Nazca Lines cover an area of 500 square kilometres (190 square miles); the longest is 8 kilometres (5 miles) long. Some align with the setting Sun on key days such as the winter solstice, the shortest day of the year. The builders may have plotted the lines from nearby hills. The shapes are impossible to see from the desert floor.

Line aligns with the setting sun

Darker rocks pushed to the side

MYSTERIOUS LINES

The huge drawings the Nazca created in the desert show geometric shapes and lines, but also animals, birds, flowers and trees. They made the lines by removing the reddish pebbles from the desert floor to uncover the whitish ground beneath. The lines have been preserved for centuries in the dry conditions. The Nazca may have planned them by studying the ground from low foothills nearby. The purpose of the lines remains a mystery after many centuries. Some people have even claimed that they were intended to guide aliens in spaceships.

TECHNICAL SPECS

- The Nazca Desert is one of the driest places in the world, so the lines have not been washed away.
- The creation of the lines exposed a sublayer of soil that contains high levels of lime. The lime hardened in the sun's heat, helping to preserve the lines.
- The largest shape is 200 metres (660 feet) across. For centuries people thought the shapes could only be seen from the air, but in fact they can be seen clearly from the nearby hilltops.
- The Nazca Lines were probably carved using simple tools like wooden stakes.

TRANSPORT

Reed boats known as balsa are still used on Lake Titicaca, in the highlands of modern-day Bolivia.

Unlike other ancient cultures, the Aztecs, Inca and Maya did not develop a wheel for transport. Wheeled vehicles would have been of limited use in the mountains or forests. Neither did they have horses for riding. Most journeys were made on foot or by boat, especially across lakes or around the coast.

The Maya and Aztecs made canoes from hollowed-out tree trunks. In the Aztec capital, Tenochtitlán, the island city was crisscrossed by canals that were crowded with canoes. Families moored canoes behind their homes.

REED BOATS

Timber was in short supply, so boats were often made from reeds that grew around lakes. The builders trimmed and bound reeds into tight bundles that they tied together to form a boat. The reeds made the boats light and strong. They were shaped so that each end of the boat was curved to help it move through the water more easily. Another form of transport was the llama. The Inca used llamas to carry loads up steep mountainsides.

TECHNICAL SPECS

- Larger reed boats could be up to 6 metres (20 feet) long. They had wooden masts and reed sails.
- In 1947 the Norwegian Thor Heyerdahl crossed the Pacific Ocean in a reed raft based on Inca designs. He believed ancient South Americans traded with the islands of the South Pacific.
- The Aztec used wheels on toys but not on vehicles.
- The Inca prized llamas so highly they did not kill them for meat.

Llamas were used by the Inca for carrying loads, and for their wool, which the Inca wove into clothes and blankets.

INCA ROADS AND BRIDGES

The heart of the Inca Empire was the imperial city of Cusco. Every road led directly to Cusco. Oddly for a civilisation that never used the wheel, the Inca still built a well-developed and extensive road system. They were master builders, and used their skill to build roads up steep mountainsides and to put bridges across deep valleys.

Inca roads used shallow steps to climb up hillsides; on steeper slopes, the roads zigzagged back and forth.

Inca roads crossed deep ravines by suspension bridges made of cables of twisted plant fibres.

COMMUNICATIONS NETWORK

The two main road systems ran from north to south. El Camino de la Costa ran along the Pacific Ocean for 4,000 kilometres (2,500 miles). Inland, the Camino Real, or Royal Way, ran through the Andes from Ecuador south to Argentina, via Cusco. The two were linked by a system of smaller roads. *Chasquis* (messengers) ran in relays with messages to and from Cusco. The Inca army also used the roads to march to the corners of the empire. Ordinary people were not allowed to use the roads in case they slowed down official messengers.

TECHNICAL SPECS

- The Camino Real was made from flat stones, while the coastal road was paved with clay bricks.
- The coastal road was up to 5 metres (15 feet) wide. The mountain road was narrower. It followed the shape of the land.
- The network of royal messengers could cover 320 kilometres (200 miles) a day.
- The Inca plaited branches between cables to form a bridge. Two more cables acted as guard rails.
- The bridge across Apurimac Canyon on the Camino Real was 36 metres (120 feet) above the river below.

ASTRONOMY

El Caracol at Chichén Itzá was used to study the sky. It aligned with the movements of the planet Venus.

The Maya believed their gods lived in the sky, so they based their lives on interpreting what they saw there. Their astronomers worked out the cycles of heavenly events. The Aztecs and Inca were also keen astronomers. The Sun and Moon played an important role in their ceremonies and rituals.

The Maya used the cycles of the Sun and Moon to predict the future. Priests told rulers the best times for actions, such as going to war. The Maya also studied the planets, particularly Venus and Mars. They had the most advanced calendar of the ancient Americans.

ALIGNMENT WITH THE SUN

Like the Maya, the Aztecs aligned temples and pyramids with the summer and winter solstices. The Inca also worked out the time of the solstices. These told them when to plant crops.

TECHNICAL SPECS

- The Aztecs planned the chief pyramids in Tenochtitlán so the Sun's rays passed between them on the spring equinox, 21 March.
- The Maya worked out that a lunar month is 29.5302 days long. The precise length is 29.53059 days.
- The Maya could predict solar eclipses, but not where they would be visible.
- The Hitching Post of the Sun at Machu Picchu indicates the two equinoxes. The Sun is directly above the stone pillar on 21 March and 23 September, so the pillar casts no shadow at noon.

Machu Picchu was a sacred Inca city where priests performed ceremonies related to the Sun.

CALENDARS

The Mayan calendar is the most famous creation of the Maya. In December 2012, it made headline news. According to the Mayan calendar, 21 December was the end of a cycle, and some people waited to see if the world would end on that day. The Aztecs adopted the Mayan calendar but gave the days and months Aztec names.

This Maya stone carving is a representation of the calendar used for 'long counts', which was made up of cycles.

In this carving of the solar calendar, the Mayan god of time is surrounded by the names of the months.

TECHNICAL SPECS

- The Maya believed that anyone born on one of the five unlucky days was cursed.
- The Mayan calendar began on 13 August, 3114 BCE. No one knows why they chose that date.
- The Maya and Aztecs thought cycles followed each other.
- The sacred calendar had two wheels, one with 13 numbers and the other with 20 named days. The wheels turned to match a number with a day.
- At the end of a cycle, the Aztecs let all their fires go out. The priests killed a human sacrifice and removed his heart. A priest lit a fire inside the empty chest, which was used to relight all the other fires.

COMPLEX CALENDARS

There were three Mayan calendars. The first was based on a sacred year of 260 days. It had two different simultaneous weeks: a numbered week of 13 days and a named week of 20 days. The second calendar was based on the solar year and was used by farmers. It had 18 months of 20 days, with five unlucky extra days to make a year of 365 days. A third calendar was used for 'long counts' made up of cycles. The longest cycle was an '*alautun*' of 23,040,000,000 days. Both the Maya and Aztecs feared the end of a cycle as an unlucky time.

WRITING

The Inca tied individual knotted strings onto a cord to create *quipu* records – but today no one knows how to read the strings.

The Maya and the Aztecs both developed a system of writing using hieroglyph characters, a little like those of the ancient Egyptians. The characters were carved in stone or written in documents. Both peoples devised counting systems that used base 20. The Inca never developed a writing system. They kept records using *quipu*, which were knotted strings.

Mayan writing had around 850 hieroglyphs. It was difficult to read. Each symbol stood for a word or part of a word, but could also stand for an idea or a sound. The Maya wrote on stone and in books called codices. The Aztecs also used hieroglyphs, but few people could read. Both the Maya and the Aztecs used symbols for numbers.

INCA QUIPU

Inca quipu were knotted strings of various thicknesses and colours. The information recorded varied according to the type of knot, the colour and the position of the strings.

TECHNICAL SPECS

- The paper used in codices was made from the fibres of the maguey cactus plant. The folded pages were bound in animal skin.
- The Maya wrote in codices using fine brushes of animal hair. They kept ink in conch shells cut in half. Four codices still exist.
- The Inca used quipu to keep records of taxes, population numbers and business deals.
- Trained accountants created and read quipu. Some quipu had more than 2,000 strings.
- To indicate that something was far away, the Aztecs drew a glyph closer to the top of a page.
- Mayan number symbols were arranged on three lines.

The Maya carved writing into stone for sacred purposes and to record important dates and events.

METALWORK

When the Spanish conquerors arrived in the Inca capital at Cusco, they found gold and silver everywhere. Ancient peoples in Peru started to make objects out of gold 3,000 years ago. The Moche of northern Peru were probably the first American people to cast metal, in around 100 CE.

Gold and silver were plentiful in Peru. People collected metals by sifting river gravel in trays. Flecks of metal were easy to spot. The Inca also dug some shallow mines.

Inca goldsmiths cast this gold figure as a handle for a knife used to sacrifice animals in religious rituals.

SPREADING SKILLS

The Moche were skilled metalworkers. They cast objects by pouring molten metal into moulds. The technique spread north, reaching Mesoamerica in about 900 CE.

GOLD WORKERS

Goldsmiths were important members of Aztec society. They cast objects using the 'lost-wax' method. The Inca both cast gold and also used cold working. This involved beating the gold into thin sheets that could then be shaped and soldered together to form hollow objects.

TECHNICAL SPECS

- The Moche developed a method of adding a thin layer of gold – gold plate – to copper. They dissolved gold in acid, then placed a copper object in the liquid. Gold coated the copper and was heated to make it bind permanently.
- The Inca called gold 'the sweat of the Sun' and silver 'the tears of the Moon'.
- Inca and Mesoamerican smiths used gold, silver and copper, with some tin, lead and platinum. They did not use iron.
- Craftsmen made the earliest-known goldwork in Peru around 3,000 years ago.
- The Inca smelted metals in clay furnaces with holes in the front. These allowed a flow of air to raise the heat of the fire to melt metals.

An Inca craftsman made this gold figurine. In Cusco, the Inca 'planted' gold and silver corncobs in a garden.

WEAPONS AND WARFARE

The Aztecs, Inca and Maya were warring peoples. They expanded their territory by going to war against their neighbours. Warriors were an elite in their societies. Another important reason to go to war was to capture prisoners for sacrifice to keep the gods happy.

All Mesoamerican males served in the army from the age of 17. They fought with wooden clubs and spears

This clay model of a warrior was made in around 600 CE by the Zapotec people who lived in Mexico.

TECHNICAL SPECS

- Aztec warriors carried a wooden *maquahuitl* (war club). It was 76 centimetres (30 inches) long and had grooved sides set with obsidian stone blades.
- The *atlatl* helped throw spears over 90 metres (300 feet). It was a wooden shaft with a handle on one end and a cup on the other, into which the end of the spear fitted.
- Warriors used flint to make sharp knives.
- Despite being well trained and large, both the Inca and Aztec armies were easily defeated by a tiny number of Spaniards. The Spaniards had guns, steel swords and horses, which the Inca and Aztecs had never seen.

This carving shows a Maya warrior in a helmet decorated with feathers. Feathers were a symbol of high status.

tipped with obsidian (a black rock; Aztec) or bronze (Inca). The Inca used catapults made from hide or wood to throw rocks. They also threw *bolas*, which were leather straps with rocks tied at the ends. When thrown at an enemy, the bolas wrapped around his legs and tripped him up.

ARMOUR AND SHIELDS

Warriors wore quilted cotton tunics. Most shields and helmets were made from wood, but the Aztecs made shields from jaguar skin and brightly coloured tropical feathers.

MEDICINE

This 20th-century painting shows Ixcuina, the Aztec goddess believed to look after women in childbirth.

In Mesoamerica and the Andes, people believed the gods made them ill if they did something to make them angry. But although healers called on the gods for help, they also understood a lot about how the human body works. They used medicinal plants to cure different ailments. Cures were a mixture of magic, offerings to please the gods and practical medicine.

The Aztecs and the Inca performed surgery with knives made from flint or obsidian. They stitched wounds with human hair or vegetable fibres, using needles made from bone. Inca surgeons bored holes in skulls to relieve headaches and could amputate limbs if necessary.

REMEDIES AND PREVENTION

The Aztecs used plants as remedies. They thought tobacco cleared the head and the coca plant deadened pain. They grew medicinal plants in botanical gardens. The Aztecs took care of their mouths. After eating, they rinsed their mouths with water and used thorns as toothpicks.

TECHNICAL SPECS

- Healers mended broken limbs by joining the broken ends of a bone together. They applied a poultice of plant root and held the limb in place with wooden splints.
- People removed tartar from their teeth with charcoal and salt water, or a mixture of alum, salt, chilli and cochineal.
- The Inca chewed coca leaves to help combat altitude sickness.
- Quinine comes from a Peruvian tree. Ancient peoples used it to prevent and treat the disease malaria; it is used for the same purpose today.
- The Spaniards brought the disease smallpox. Native peoples had no immunity, so it killed millions.

In this 16th-century image, an Aztec midwife gives a herbal remedy to a woman who has just given birth.

TEXTILES

Some of the most remarkable textiles in South America were some of the earliest. The Paracas people, who lived in the Andes from about 900 BCE to 400 CE, wove elaborate designs into their cloth. For the Inca who followed them in Peru, textiles were their most valuable possessions. They were more valuable than gold.

A descendant of the Inca weaves a colourful textile on a backstrap loom. The long threads are the warp threads.

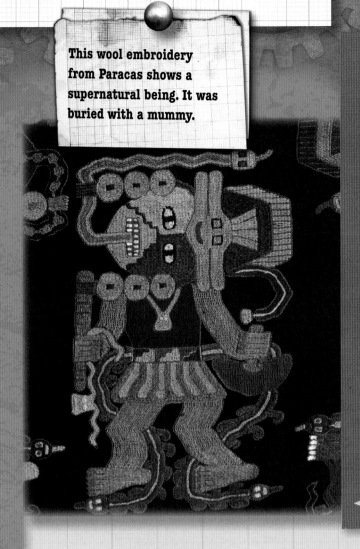

This wool embroidery from Paracas shows a supernatural being. It was buried with a mummy.

TECHNICAL SPECS

- In Paracas, cloth was dyed with bright colours such as indigo (blue) and pink.
- Paracas cloth was often heavily embroidered. People used it to wrap dead bodies before they were buried.
- One ancient Peruvian noble was buried with 135 kilograms (300 pounds) of cotton in his grave.
- Cochineal beetles, which live on cactus plants, produce red dye. To make 500 grams (1 pound) of dye required 70,000 beetles.
- Llamas and alpacas produced a glossy wool, but the finest wool came from their relative, the wild vicuña.

The Paracas people wove textiles from the wool of llamas and alpacas and from plant fibres, such as cotton. Designs woven into the cloth illustrated the tribe's religious beliefs. Some textiles are up to 35 metres (115 feet) long: many workers would have been needed to produce them.

BACKSTRAP LOOM

Andean peoples wove on a backstrap loom. One end of the warp threads was attached to a wooden bar that was hung on a tree or post. The other end was strapped around the weaver's back. The weaver altered the tautness of the yarn by leaning back as she passed the weft (sideways) thread through the warp (longways) threads.

POTTERY

The Mesoamericans and Inca were skilled potters, but they did not use potters' wheels or kilns (ovens). Every vessel was shaped by hand. The pots were richly decorated using a variety of techniques. The best ceramics were used for religious ceremonies or by the rich.

Potters in both the Andes and Mesoamerica made pots by shaping coils of clay, by moulding clay or by carving blocks of clay. Mesoamerican potters often produced slipware. Before a pot was fired, they decorated it with semi-liquid clay, known as slip. They used different coloured slips to paint decoration on the pot. Instead of using kilns,

The Moche made 'portrait vessels', which showed people or gods. Other designs showed animals.

Mimbres potters crushed plants and rocks to make paint. They made brushes from feathers and twigs.

early American potters fired (heated) their pots in a fire. They made pottery known as blackware by controlling how much oxygen the pot received as it was fired.

DISTINCTIVE POTTERY

Some of the most distinctive pottery was made by the Moche of northern Peru. They made pots in complex human and animal forms. The pots had U-shaped 'stirrup' spouts. From the ninth century CE, the Mogollon people of Arizona and New Mexico produced a distinctive black-on-white pottery, known as Mimbres. It is notable for its distinctive decoration featuring elaborate geometric designs.

TECHNICAL SPECS

- The Inca used moulds to make basic pots such as the *aryballos* jar. The jar had a conical base, a tall, flared neck and handles on the sides.
- Most Inca pottery was polished red, with geometric patterns in red, white and black.
- Whistling water jars were double vessels connected by hollow tubes. As water flowed from one vessel it pushed air out of the other through a whistle. Some whistling jars were made in the shape of the quetzal, a bird sacred to both the Aztecs and the Maya.
- The Maya covered their pots with a coloured plaster called stucco.
- The Mogollon people often buried Mimbres pots with the dead. They first 'killed' the pots by punching a hole through their base.

TIMELINE

BCE

3114 — The Mayan calendar begins on 13 August.

c.3000 — Pottery first appears in the Americas, in what are now Colombia and Ecuador.

c.1150 — The Olmec culture appears in Mexico.

c.900 — The Olmec build the first pyramid in America, at La Venta.

c.800 — The Paracas culture appears in Peru; it is famed for its textiles.

c.300 — The earliest stages of Mayan culture appear in Mesoamerica.

c.300 — An unknown people begins building the great city of Teotihuacán in central Mexico.

c.100 — The Paracas culture disappears.

CE

c.100 — The Olmec culture in Mexico declines.

c.100 — The Moche of northern Peru begin to cast objects in metal.

c.400 — The Nazca of Peru begin drawing huge designs in the desert.

c.500 — The Maya build the city of Tikal, which has many tall pyramids.

c.600 — The Maya civilisation reaches its height.

c.600 — Teotihuacán is abandoned for unknown reasons.

c.600 — Cahokia is founded in Illinois in the United States.

c.850 — The Maya civilisation begins a decline.

899 — The Maya abandon the city of Tikal.

c.900 — The Pueblo build adobe communal dwellings in Chaco Canyon.

c.900	Casting techniques reach Mesoamerica.
c.1000	The Mogollon culture reaches its classic phase, producing distinctive black-and-white Mimbres pottery.
c.1100	The Toltec emerge in Mexico, building a capital at Tula.
c.1100	At its peak, Cahokia in Illinois has 100 mounds.
c.1100	The Anasazi build cliff homes at Mesa Verde and Canyon de Chelly, in the United States.
c.1200	The Aztecs move into central Mexico from an origin further to the north.
c.1200	The first Inca emperor, Manco Cápac, founds an empire from Cusco in the Andes.
1325	The Aztecs begin their rise to power, and build their capital Tenochtitlán in the middle of a shallow lake.
1438	The Inca build the sacred city of Machu Picchu in a remote mountaintop location.
c.1470	The Inca conquer the neighbouring Chimu culture.
1492	European explorer Christopher Columbus crosses the Atlantic and lands on Hispaniola in the Caribbean, marking European contact with the Americas.
1498	Columbus lands on mainland America.
1517	The first Spaniards land in Mexico, on the Yucatán Peninsula. They introduce illnesses, such as smallpox, to which native peoples have no immunity; within a century, these diseases devastate the population of Mesoamerica.
1519	Spanish conquistador Hernán Cortés lands in Mexico and begins to conquer the Aztec Empire.
1521	Cortés destroys the Aztec capital at Tenochtitlán; it will be rebuilt as Mexico City.

GLOSSARY

aqueduct A pipe or channel that carries water over a long distance.

canal An artificial waterway.

cast To make objects by pouring molten metal into a mould.

causeway A raised roadway across a lake or marsh.

chinampa An artificial island built in a shallow lake for use as a 'floating garden'.

codices (sing. codex) Early forms of books, with pages sewn together.

elite A small group of privileged people.

embroider To sew a design onto a piece of cloth with coloured thread.

empire A large territory ruled by an emperor or empress.

furnace A very hot oven used to fire clay or to melt metals.

hieroglyph A picture or symbol used for writing.

irrigation Artificially watering fields in order to grow crops.

kiln An oven used to harden pottery or bake bricks.

'lost-wax' method A way of making metal objects in which molten metal is poured into a clay mould holding a wax model of the finished object.

Mesoamerica An area inhabited by similar cultures that included parts of Mexico, Guatemala, Honduras, Belize, El Salvador and Nicaragua.

pueblo A communal building made of adobe in the southwest of the United States; the term also describes the peoples who built them.

pyramid A four-sided structure that tapers to a point.

slip A layer of liquid clay used to decorate pottery.

smelt To extract a metal from its ore by heating it.

solder To join metals by melting an alloy to bind them together.

staple A food that makes up the major part of a diet.

terrace A flat bank of earth with steep sides.

terracotta A brownish-red fired clay.

wattle and daub A building material made from a lattice of wood covered in mud.

weir A low dam built across a river.

ziggurat A pyramid that rises in steps to a flat top.

FURTHER INFORMATION

BOOKS

Aztec, Inca and Maya (Eyewitness Books). DK Publishing, 2011.

Clarke, Catriona. *Aztecs* (Usborne Beginners). Usborne Publishing, 2007.

Deary, Terry. *The Angry Aztecs* (Horrible Histories). Scholastic, 2008.

Deary, Terry. *The Incredible Incas* (Horrible Histories). Scholastic, 2008.

Kelly, Tracey. *The Maya* (Great Civilisations). Franklin Watts, 2014.

Thomson, Ruth. *Aztecs* (Craft Topics). Franklin Watts, 2008.

WEBSITES

www.civilization.ca/maya/
Canadian Museum of Civilization introduction to the Maya: Secrets of their World.

www.ancientworlds.net/aw/
Article/729894
Ancientworlds.com guide to Inca technology, with links.

www.britishmuseum.org/explore/
cultures/the_americas/aztecs_mexica.
aspx
British Museum introduction to the culture of the Aztecs.

INDEX